THE BOOK
OF
THE ROYAL YEAR

First published in Great Britain, 1987
by Michael O'Mara Books Limited
20 Queen Anne Street, London W1N 9FB
in association with
Independent Television News Limited

Published by SUMMIT BOOKS
A Division of Simon & Schuster, Inc.
Simon & Schuster Building, Rockefeller Center
1230 Avenue of the Americas, New York, NY 10020

SUMMIT BOOKS and colophon are trademarks of
Simon & Schuster, Inc.

Designed by Martin Bristow

Printed and bound by Mohndruck,
Gütersloh, West Germany

10 9 8 7 6 5 4 3 2 1

Library of Congress Catalog Card Number
87-10223

ISBN 0-671-64836-5

Previous page: The Queen in Berlin on 26 May 1987
This page: The Prince and Princess of Wales enjoy the spectacular view of Lisbon from the Castle of St George during their visit to Portugal in February 1987

THE BOOK OF THE ROYAL YEAR

PHOTOGRAPHED BY TIM GRAHAM

SUMMIT BOOKS
New York

THE WEDDING OF THE DUKE
AND DUCHESS OF YORK

23 July 1986

On Wednesday, 23 July 1986, Prince Andrew and Sarah Ferguson were married at Westminster Abbey. That morning the Queen had created Prince Andrew Duke of York, Earl of Inverness and Baron of Killyleagh. The royal bridegroom was escorted to the Abbey by his brother and sponsor, Prince Edward, and was soon to face the world with his bride – as the Duke and Duchess of York.

It was a happy day for everyone. The bride and groom waved to the crowds on their return journey to Buckingham Palace where they and the Royal Family assembled on the balcony. At the people's bidding the Duke kissed his bride amid tumultuous cheers. The bridal party on the balcony consisted of (left to right) Mrs Susan Ferguson, Prince Charles, Princess Margaret, the Princess of Wales holding Prince Henry, Major Ronald Ferguson (bride's father), Mrs Susan Barrantes (bride's mother), the bride and groom, Prince Edward, the Queen Mother, the Queen, the Duke of Edinburgh, Princess Anne, Captain Mark Phillips, Mrs Jane Makim (bride's sister), Alexander Makim, Lady Elmhirst and the Hon. Mrs Doreen Wright (bride's grandmothers). Children: Seamus Makim, Andrew Ferguson, Peter Phillips, Lady Rosanagh Innes-Ker, Zara Phillips, Laura Fellowes, Prince William, Alice Ferguson, Lady Davina Windsor and Lady Rose Windsor.

The Going Away amid a shower of rose petals. (Above and opposite) The royal couple left Buckingham Palace in an open State Landau. They were driven to Chelsea Barracks where a helicopter took them to Heathrow Airport for a flight to the Azores to join HMY Britannia. (Right) After a five-day cruise the couple sailed back to join the Royal Family for Cowes Week on the Isle of Wight.

The day after the wedding, 24 July, saw the Prince and Princess of Wales on a two-day visit to the Shetland Islands, north of Scot'and. (Opposite and right) In Lerwick, the capital, the Prince and Princess visited the Town Hall and spoke to local fishermen who were dressed as Vikings during celebrations for their 'Fire Festival'. (Above) The following day the couple travelled to the coastal village of Aith, northwest of Lerwick, where the Princess named a new Royal National Lifeboat Institution (RNLI) lifeboat Snolda.

On the first day of August the Princess of Wales, as Colonel in Chief, visited the Royal Hampshire Regiment at Tidworth in Hampshire where she presented new colours to the 1st Battalion. She wore the regimental brooch presented to her in October 1985 when she visited the regiment during their term in West Berlin.

THE QUEEN MOTHER'S BIRTHDAY

4 August 1986

August 4 is a special day in the Royal Family for it is the Queen Mother's birthday. This year she was 86 and, as always, made her customary appearance outside her home at Clarence House in London, to the delight of the enthusiastic crowd of well-wishers.

The Queen Mother was joined by her family at Clarence House where a celebration lunch was held. The previous day, Sunday, had been spent at Sandringham with the Queen. The Royal Family then drove to London where they were joined by the Duke and Duchess of York (left) who had interrupted their extended honeymoon for the occasion. The Princess of Wales (right) arrived at Clarence House clutching a bunch of flowers for her husband's grandmother.

At the start of her annual holiday at Balmoral in Scotland, the Queen (left) boards the royal yacht at Southampton. As the yacht sets sail (above) she waves, with her grandchildren Peter and Zara Phillips, to the crowds on the dockside. (Right) On 12 August Prince Charles returned from a holiday in Majorca to join the royal cruise and to enjoy some salmon fishing. He is seen here three days later being welcomed by the Queen Mother at Scrabster. The following day, 16 August, the Queen with the Duke and Duchess of York (above right and far right) visited the Port of Aberdeen. The Queen unveiled a plaque to celebrate the Port's 850th Anniversary. This marked the end of the cruise on Britannia as the Royal Family travelled on to Balmoral for the rest of their holiday.

Welcome to Scotland. The Princess of Wales arrived at Aberdeen Airport on 16 August with Prince William and Prince Henry who is given a helping hand. They had just returned from a few days in Majorca as guests of the King and Queen of Spain. Meanwhile, HMY Britannia had cruised to the Western Isles and on 15 August arrived at Scrabster where the Queen (right) and Prince Charles (previous page) were greeted by the Queen Mother who then entertained her family to lunch at nearby Castle of Mey. (Below) Prince Henry arrives at Heathrow Airport after the flight home from Aberdeen at the end of his Scottish holiday.

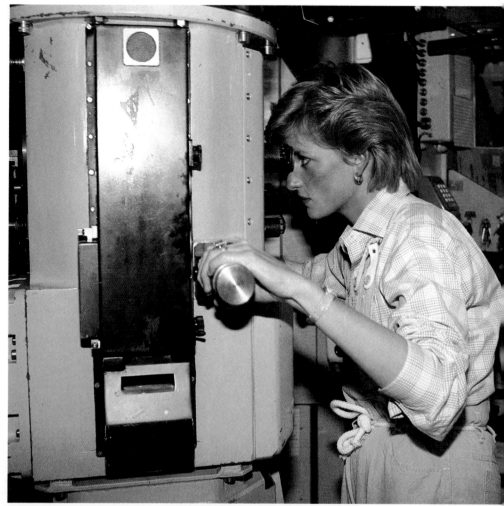

During her holiday at Balmoral the Princess of Wales visited Faslane, the naval submarine base and home of the British Polaris Fleet on the Firth of Clyde. Here she boarded HMS Trafalgar *(this page and overleaf), one of Britain's most modern submarines and part of NATO's strike force. The Princess spoke to members of the crew of 130 officers and men and viewed nearby vessels through the periscope. The visit on 22 August was kept top secret.*

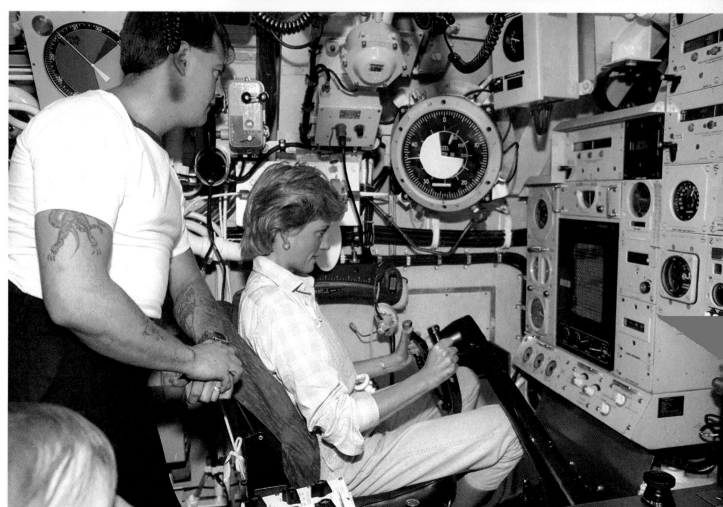

The Duke and Duchess of York were soon joining the 'Royal Firm' and participating in their share of engagements. Their first official engagement (left) was at Aycliffe Special School in County Durham on 12 September. The Duke is patron of the school and much concerned with its work for problem children. The couple's first overseas engagement was a visit to the Netherlands at the invitation of Queen Beatrix to attend the inauguration ceremony for the £2 billion Storm Surge Barrier in the River Oosterschelde in Zeeland (right). They were met at the airport (below left) by Crown Prince Willem Alexander. The morning after the ceremony, on 4 October, the couple were driven from The Hague to St Mary's Anglican Church – a Seamen's Mission Church – in Rotterdam to attend a service where the Duke read the lesson. (Below right) The Duchess chose a brown check suit and matching brown hat for the occasion.

THE QUEEN'S VISIT TO CHINA AND HONG KONG

12-23 October 1986

On Sunday, 12 October 1986, the Queen became the first British monarch to visit China. This historic visit began with an official welcome in Peking when the Queen inspected a guard of honour with President Li Xiannian and later toured the fabulous Forbidden City, home of the ancient emperors of China.

The end of the first day in China was marked by a State Banquet in the Great Hall of the People. Below is the Queen's place setting at the 10-course banquet which included sea slug, shark's fin and dragon's eyes (fruit). The following day (right) the Queen and Prince Philip visited the Great Wall of China which dates back over 2,000 years and stretches 3,930 miles with its branches and spurs. The section the royal couple walked at Badaling shows fine military architecture of the Ming period which protected the way into Peking.

On Thursday, 16 October, after spending the previous day in Shanghai, the Queen flew inland to Xian where she viewed the army of terracotta figures built 2,000 years ago to guard the tomb of the emperor, Qin Shihuang. Nearly 7,000 life-size warriors were made and those so far excavated stand in a large vault in order of rank. The site is truly one of the archeological wonders of the world. (Far right) On 18 October the royal party arrived in Canton, the final stop on the 3,000-mile tour of China. On her arrival the Queen was presented with a bouquet by the grandson of the local governor.

During the afternoon of her day in
Canton the Queen was given a wonderful
welcome by 300 children at the Children's
Palace, a centre of learning and
recreation set in a park. Even the rain did
not spoil this enchanting occasion.

After a leisurely two-day cruise down the Pearl River and along the South China Coast the Queen and Prince Philip arrived in Hong Kong. It was a spectacular scene as the royal yacht sailed into Victoria Harbour to a fly-past and 21-gun salute. The Queen disembarked and was received by the Governor of Hong Kong and his wife Lady Youde (left). The Queen inspected a guard of honour of the Gurkhas during the arrival ceremony. A highlight of her two days in Hong Kong was a visit to the races (above). Sir Michael Sandberg, Chairman of the Royal Jockey Club, and Lady Sandberg showed the royal couple round Sha Tin Racecourse and presented the Queen with a commemorative gift. An exciting firework display in the Harbour marked the end of the Queen's visit before she flew back to London the following morning. The Duke of Edinburgh, however, remained in Hong Kong to review the Seventh Duke of Edinburgh's Own Gurkha Rifles at the Kyenum Barracks before the battalion was to be disbanded. The Duke is seen greeting the families of the men serving in Hong Kong (right).

THE VISIT OF THE PRINCE AND PRINCESS OF WALES TO THE MIDDLE EAST

10-19 November 1986

On 10 November the Prince and Princess of Wales left RAF Brize Norton and flew to Oman to start a nine-day tour of Oman, Qatar, Bahrain and Saudi Arabia. It was a business trip in a region where Britain had much influence until 1971. Today Britain enjoys a healthy trading surplus with the Gulf States and Prince Charles was to help promote this trading relationship.

On 11 November the Prince and Princess left HMY Britannia *and went ashore to Muscat in Oman where they were welcomed by Sultan Qaboos bin Said Al Said. During the arrival ceremony (right) Prince Charles inspected a guard of honour. (Below left and below) The Sultan opened his opulent and beautiful palace specially for the royal couple – something that had not been done before.*

After the Sultan's warm welcome the royal couple separated and the Princess of Wales visited the Oman Women's Association. Here the women demonstrated their customary marriage ritual and showed the Princess a traditional Omani house (left).

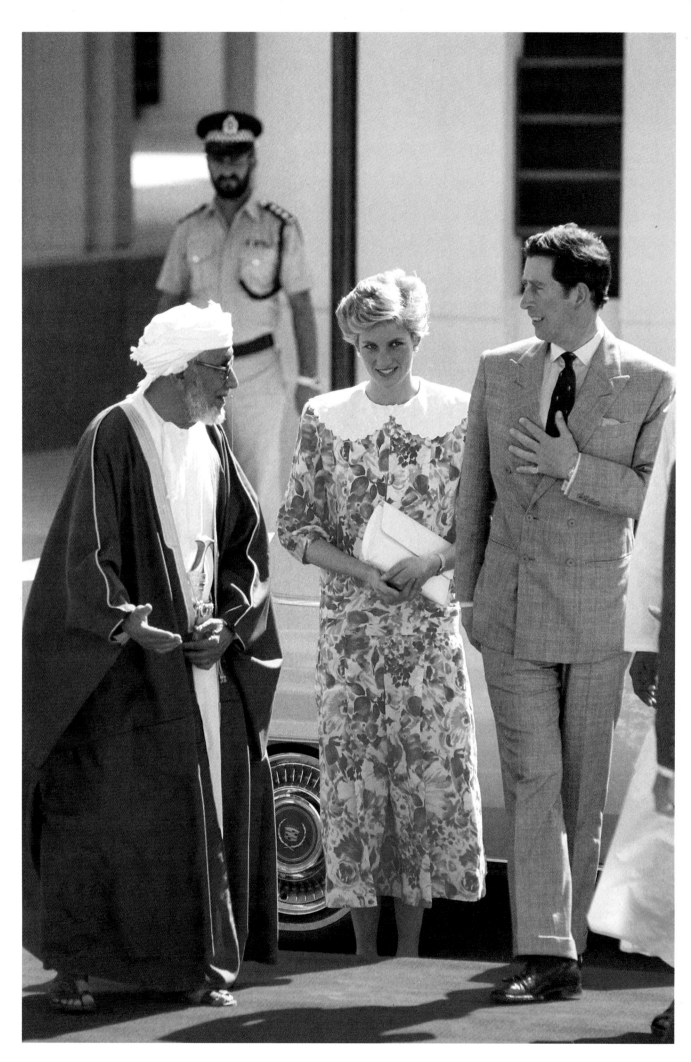

On Wednesday, 12 November, the royal couple visited Sultan Qaboos University (far left) where the Princess had the opportunity of talking to the female students all in national dress (left), who are strictly segregated from the male students. This large and modern campus was built by British engineers. After a private lunch the Princess watched her husband play polo (below).

During their visit to Qatar the Prince and Princess were unexpectedly invited to a special banquet together by the Amir. The Princess was to attend the all-male banquet as a gesture to celebrate her husband's 38th birthday on 14 November. For this banquet she wore a stunning dress designed by Catherine Walker. The following afternoon (below) the royal couple were taken on an excursion to the desert.

The desert entertainment in Qatar consisted of demonstrations of camel racing and hawking. The couple's visit was short but they did not leave before greeting the British crowd who had turned out to see them. The Princess wore a calf-length dress just within the limits but far shorter than anything worn by the Queen during her visit to the Gulf in 1979.

On Sunday, 16 November, the couple flew to Bahrain and that evening they were entertained by the Amir at a State Banquet. The Princess wore a stunning Emanuel dress for the occasion. Earlier in the day (below) the Princess wore another Emanuel outfit when she and Prince Charles were welcomed by the Amir.

From Bahrain the Prince and Princess of Wales flew to Riyadh in Saudi Arabia where one of the highlights of the visit was undoubtedly the exotic luncheon in the desert at Thumanah with an elaborate programme of entertainment which included Arab horses, falcons, camels, dancing tribesmen and hypnotic drum beating.

King Fahd went out of his way to entertain the Prince and Princess of Wales royally in the absence of the Crown Prince. The couple attended a State audience at one of his many palaces. The Princess looked radiant in her tiara and evening dress but was to dine separately with the royal princesses. The last day of the tour, 19 November, started with a formal departure at Riyadh Airport (above right and right) as the Prince and Princess flew to Jedda to join HMY Britannia.

The Royal Family always give their support to good causes and on 26 November the Duchess of Kent, as Controller Commandant of the Women's Royal Army Corps, visited the London Provost Company of the Royal Military Police (left). The following day the Princess of Wales (below) attended the launch of the Anti-Drugs Campaign where she presented awards for the Westminster City Council at the Rock Garden Restaurant in Covent Garden. Later that day (right) there was a rare opportunity to see Lady Davina and Lady Rose (front), daughters of the Duke and Duchess of Gloucester, when they attended a Royal Gala Performance of 'The Lion, the Witch and the Wardrobe' with their parents at the Westminster Theatre in London.

On 3 December the Duchess of York
(below left) opened a charity fair at the
Park Lane Hotel in London. Later in the
week Princess Anne visited Nottingham
where she ended a busy day at a
Reception in the County Hall which was
followed by a Gala Evening at the Theatre
Royal (left). On 9 December Prince and
Princess Michael of Kent (right) attended
the SPARKS Charity Tennis Ball at the
Hilton Hotel in London. (Below right) The
Duchess of York attended Christmas
Carols with the Stars held in aid of the
Leukemia Research Fund at the Royal
Albert Hall in London on 17 December.

At the end of the Christmas term Prince William's nursery school performed a nativity play in which the young Prince played the innkeeper (opposite above and right). The Princess of Wales had taken him to school earlier in the day (far left) and returned later to attend the performance. She was greeted by young admirers outside the school (opposite below). On 15 January, the following term, Prince William began at his pre-prep school (below left) on a cold, snowy morning. Wetherby School is only a short drive from Kensington Palace and has 120 boys between the ages of 4 ½ and 8. Prince William returned home at the end of his first morning (below right) before starting full time the next day.

On 11 February the Prince and Princess of Wales flew to Portugal on a four-day visit to help promote British exports and to enhance relations between the two countries. Prince Charles landed an aircraft of the Queen's Flight at Lisbon (above) where the couple started their tour (below and right). That evening they attended a banquet hosted by President Cavaro Silva. The following day (opposite) the royal couple visited Jerónimos Monastery which was built by Manuel I to the glory of the Portuguese navigators at the beginning of the sixteenth century. Sculptors carved Christian symbols together with those from the Portuguese conquests at sea which resulted in a striking and original style.

The morning of Thursday the 12th ended with a visit to the sailing vessel Creoula (opposite page right) at Docado. The evening was spent at a performance of a modern ballet (right) by the Gulbenkian Ballet Company. The Princess of Wales wore a satin jacket with a black skirt and bow tie. The following morning the royal couple visited Sintra National Palace (opposite page left) before departing for Oporto where they attended a farewell banquet (left and below) hosted by the Prime Minister at the Bolsa Palace. Members of the Port Wine Fraternity lined the entrance to the Palace dressed in their traditional red robes.

On 17 February the Prince and Princess of Wales joined the Duke and Duchess of York for a skiing holiday in Klosters in Switzerland. The Duke and Duchess had already settled into the rented chalet the four were to share at nearby Wolfgang. The local Tourist Director organized a photocall for the hundred or so members of the press who had gathered in Klosters. During the photocall the Princess of Wales jokingly accused the Duchess of York of standing on her skis which resulted in some gentle pushing. The Princess sported a striking new ski suit this year while her brother-in-law, the Duke of York, appropriately wore a bobble hat with a helicopter motif.

The busy royal calendar in February saw
the Duchess of York (far left above), as
patron, visiting the National Association
of Flower Arrangement Societies' show at
Queensway West in London. Two days
later on 5 February the Princess of Wales
(left) accompanied Prince Charles to the
Savoy Hotel in London. As patron of the
Asian Affairs Society he was attending the
Society's annual banquet. On Monday the
23rd the Princess attended a performance
of the show 'High Society' (far left below),
in aid of the Help the Hospices charity, at
the Victoria Palace Theatre in London.

The Queen with the Duke of Edinburgh
attended the Observance Service at
Westminster Abbey in London (opposite
below right) on Commonwealth Day, 9
March). On Wednesday the 11th the Queen
and the Duke attended a service at St
Paul's Cathedral for the Dedication of the
Korean War Memorial (right). They were
received on the steps of the Cathedral by
the Lord Mayor (Sir David Rowe-Ham), the
Dean (the Very Rev. Alan Webster) and the
Patron of the British Korean Veterans
Association (General Sir Anthony Farrar-
Hockley). The Queen unveiled the
Memorial which was dedicated by the
Bishop of Fulham and afterwards, with the
Duke, laid a wreath. The following day
the Duchess of York (below) planted a tree
for the first time for the Westminster Tree
and Preservation Trust in Pimlico,
London. She wore an eye-catching red
dress with the hemline above her knee.

On Saturday, 28 February, Princess Anne made her debut at steeplechasing at Kempton Park, when she rode Cnoc Na Cuille (far left, left and below). She took part in the Portlane Handicap Chase, run over 2½ miles and with 17 fences to negotiate, and came home fourth. Cnoc Na Cuille's next race with the Princess was at Sandown Park on 13 March (bottom right) in the Horse and Hound Grand Military Gold Cup. The Princess came in a disappointing eighth, but the Queen and Queen Mother (bottom left) were there to cheer her on.

The Duchess of York (left and above left) rode Aldaniti, the 1981 Grand National Winner, through the grounds of Windsor Castle on 3 March. She was participating in an attempt to raise £500,000 for the Bob Champion Cancer Trust during which some 250 people each rode Aldaniti for a mile during a five-week trek to Liverpool. Princess Anne (right and above right) took the reins of Aldaniti at the Cheltenham National Hunt Festival on 17 March. Bob Champion was to complete the final mile to Aintree before the start of the 1987 Grand National.

THE STATE VISIT OF KING FAHD

24-27 March 1987

King Fahd's visit followed the royal visit of the Prince and Princess of Wales to Saudi Arabia in November and also coincided with the completion of a large aircraft deal between Britain and Saudi Arabia.

The Prince and Princess of Wales, accompanied by the Saudi Arabian Ambassador, welcomed King Fahd on behalf of the Queen at Gatwick Airport. The royal party then travelled by train to London. The Princess of Wales chose a stylish 'hussar' suit for the occasion.

King Fahd was entertained at a banquet given by the Lord Mayor and Corporation of London at Guildhall (right) on 25 March, which was also attended by the Duke and Duchess of Gloucester. The following evening the King hosted a State Banquet at Claridge's Hotel in London. It was a truly royal occasion: (below) the Hon. Angus Ogilvy and his wife, Princess Alexandra, talk to the King; also attending were Princess Anne (opposite above left), and the Duchess of York with her husband the Duke (opposite above right). (Opposite below) King Fahd posed with the Queen and the Duke of Edinburgh for a formal photograph to mark the occasion.

On 16 April, Maundy Thursday, the Queen and the Duke of Edinburgh travelled by Royal Train to Ely where they attended the Maundy Service at the Cathedral (opposite page and above). The Queen distributed 61 Maundy purses to needy people – one for each year of her life. The Queen's Body Guard of the Yeoman of the Guard were on duty. One month later, on 13 May, the Queen and the Duke visited the Isle of Wight (left) to celebrate the 200th Anniversary of the departure for Australia of the First Fleet. The royal couple sailed from Portsmouth. They disembarked at Ryde where they had inspected crews sailing to Australia and were officially received by the Council. During the afternoon the Queen unveiled a commemorative plaque, attended a British-Australian Heritage Society Exhibition and walked through St Thomas's Square.

The Royal Family spent Easter at Windsor Castle and attended the Easter Sunday Service at St George's Chapel on 19 April: (left) the Princess of Wales with her eldest son, Prince William both in matching coats, and Peter Phillips (Princess Anne's son), and (above) the Duchess of York. Shortly after Easter, on 30 April, the Duke and Duchess of Kent left for a four-day royal tour of Sierra Leone where they represented the Queen during anniversary celebrations. They flew from RAF Northolt (right) in an aircraft of the Queen's Flight. The High Commissioner for Sierra Leone and the Special Representative of the Secretary of State for Foreign and Commonwealth Affairs received the Duke and Duchess at RAF Northolt. (Above right) The Princess of Wales on one of her many visits marked National No Smoking Day on 5 March by touring Kentish Town Health Centre in London.

THE PRINCE AND PRINCESS OF WALES' VISIT TO SPAIN

21-25 April 1987

This was the first official tour of the Prince and Princess of Wales to Spain. It was a visit full of culture with the royal couple revelling in the art and architecture of Spain. After the formal official welcome in Madrid King Juan Carlos and Queen Sophia made the visit informal and relaxed.

(Above) Princesses Elena and Christina, daughters of the King and Queen of Spain, welcome the Prince and Princess of Wales in Madrid on their arrival. (Right) The Princess attended a British fashion show in Madrid. (Opposite page) A day trip to Salamanca.

The colourful old city of Salamanca, to
the northwest of Madrid, saw the crowds
(right), and the press (top), out in force to
welcome the royal party. Dancing (above)
and singing filled the streets.

The royal party were serenaded by university students in Salamanca. The students were dressed in traditional troubadour outfits. The Princess of Wales honoured them by walking over their cloaks, which were covered in rosettes, and then by donning one of the cloaks herself.

At the end of the four-day visit the King drove the Prince and Princess some 70 miles to the city of Toledo, the ancient capital of Spain. The city sprawls over a vast crag with the fast-flowing River Tagus surrounding it (left). In a city full of architecture from every period the Cathedral (below left) is the finest Gothic monument, begun in the thirteenth century. Its single tower commands the whole city. The party wandered through the city streets (below right) visiting local shops and the market. At the end of an informal and enjoyable day the Prince and Princess took their leave of the King and Queen (opposite below) and then Prince Charles flew his wife to Granada for a private weekend at the estate of the Duke of Wellington.

On Saturday, 2 May the Duke and Duchess of York flew to Jersey where the Duchess started the prestigious Jersey International Air Race (below left). The couple saw an air display to commemorate the 50th Anniversary of Jersey Airport. In the evening the States of Jersey held a dinner at the Atlantic Hotel in their honour (below right). On Sunday the royal couple visited some cottages for pensioners and did a walkabout.

On 7 May the Duke and Duchess of York visited the Red Arrows at the Royal Air Force Central Flying School, Scampton in Lincolnshire. They were received by the Commandant and the Deputy Commandant of the school. The visit marked the opening of the twenty-third season of the Red Arrows aerobatic display team. A special display was mounted when the team flew in the formation of a heart. One of the highlights of the day for the Duchess was when she looped the loop at the controls of a Bulldog training aircraft (opposite page). She was accompanied by Squadron Leader David Walby, who taught the Duke of York and Prince Edward.

The Prince and Princess of Wales flew to
the South of France for the Cannes Film
Festival on 15 May. They were officially
welcomed at the Town Hall by the lady
Mayor of Cannes. The Princess of Wales
wore her up-to-the-minute Catherine
Walker puff-ball dress, originally seen in
Portugal, but this time she teamed it with
a smart white jacket. Later in the day the
royal couple found time to visit the British
Pavilion (opposite below right) at the
Festival. (Overleaf) The Princess looked
every inch a star herself in a beautiful silk
chiffon evening dress when she and Prince
Charles attended a gala night in honour
of Sir Alec Guinness. The royal couple also
saw the British film 'The Whales of August'
at the Palais de Festival.

The Royal Windsor Horse Show was held in mid May in Windsor Great Park. The show takes place each year and its main events include show-jumping, dressage and carriage-driving. The Royal Family always enjoy the show, and the Queen and the Duke and Duchess of York are seen here during the weekend of 16-17 May. The Duchess of York had recently been receiving lessons in carriage-driving – one of the favourite pastimes of the Duke of Edinburgh, her father-in-law – and no doubt took a keen interest in those trials as well as the other events. Prince Edward (right), although not as keen as his eldest brother and his sister, also enjoys riding.

Polo has been played by members of the Royal Family since it was introduced to England over 100 years ago. There are only four members in a polo team making it easy to organize a game. The Duke of Edinburgh was one of the top players in his day and he encouraged Prince Charles to take up the sport. The Prince of Wales began playing when he was 14. Major Ronald Ferguson, father of the Duchess of York, has managed Prince Charles's polo since the mid 1970s. Here Prince Charles plays at Smith's Lawn, Windsor, on 17 and 31 May. He is watched by the Princess of Wales and his sons, Prince William and Prince Henry – although Prince William seems to find driving an ambulance more fun (opposite above right) and after a tiring, wet afternoon Prince Henry wanted the shelter of his mother's arms (above).

During the cold and wet
weekend of 22-24 May,
Princess Anne and her
family attended the
Windsor Horse Trials.
These take place annually
in Windsor Great Park.
Princess Anne takes an
active part in organizing
this three-day event. Her
son, Peter Phillips, and her
daughter, Zara braved the
weather (opposite page) to
attend the trials with their
mother. They are both
becoming keen riders
themselves, much to the
delight of their mother
and their grandmother,
the Queen.

On 26 May the Queen and the Duke of Edinburgh flew to the Federal Republic of Germany. The Queen took the Salute at the Queen's Birthday Parade of the British Forces in Berlin. The royal couple also attended celebrations for the city's 750th Anniversary. The following morning the Queen and the Duke of Edinburgh rode in an open State Landau (opposite above left) specially sent to Berlin for the parade. During the Parade she inspected over 1,000 British troops and viewed some dazzling parades. The previous evening the royal couple had been guests of the mayor at a banquet held at the Schloss Charlottenberg (above and left).

The Derby is one of the most famous races in the world and has been taking place for 208 years. The Queen rarely misses Derby Day at the Epsom Racecourse and 3 June, this year, was no exception. In the royal party were Princess Alexandra and her husband, the Hon. Angus Ogilvy (far left above), the Duchess of York, the Prince and Princess of Wales and the Queen Mother. It was the Duchess of York's first Derby Day as part of the Royal Family and she obviously enjoyed watching the races with her sister-in-law, the Princess of Wales. The Queen dearly wishes to win the Derby one day and had a second place in 1953 with Aureole. Flat-racing, breeding horses and three-day eventing are her great hobbies.

On 23 March (above left) the Queen Mother, accompanied by the Prince and Princess of Wales, went to the Royal Film Performance of '84 Charing Cross Road' held in aid of the Cinema and Television Benevolent Fund at the Odeon in London's Leicester Square. A few weeks later the Duchess of Kent (far right below) attended the Bartres Ball held in aid of Hosanna House Trust on 19 May at the Grosvenor House in the West End of London. The Duchess of York is seen (above) on 20 May at the Grosvenor House where she attended a lunch in aid of Birthright – her stepmother is chairman of the committee. Her jacket was designed by Yves Saint Laurent and the fashion house had advertised it during the Spring under the heading of Papillon (butterfly). During a visit to the Royal Aero Club (opposite above left) on 21 May with the Duke of York when she presented the Club's Award to her father-in-law, the Duke of Edinburgh. On 1 June (opposite above right) the Duchess of York visited Christie's to attend a charity auction of art and jewelry for the Aids Crisis Trust in association with Crusaid. The following evening (left) the Duchess was present at a performance of Manon at the Royal Opera House. This was followed by a Ball at the Royal College of Art in aid of the National Society for the Prevention of Cruelty to Children. A few days later, on 9 June, Princess Michael of Kent (right) attended the Women of the World Luncheon held at the Café Royal in London.

Prince William and Prince Henry spend many of their summer weekends at Highgrove, just outside Tetbury. Only a short drive away in Prince Charles's Aston Martin (right) is the Earl of Bathurst's 3,000-acre estate at Cirencester Park with its notable five-mile avenue of chestnuts and polo ground. On Saturday, 6 June, the young princes braved the rain to watch their father play polo at Cirencester Park – Prince William (left) is seen sporting a smart umbrella (right above) and taking a dog for a walk (right below) while Prince Henry follows obediently (far right above). Prince Charles made his debut into high-goal polo playing for the Hon. Mark Vestey's team, Foxcote, based at Cirencester.

The Queen, the Duke of Edinburgh, the Princess of Wales with Prince William and Prince Henry, and the Duke and the Duchess of York all watched Prince Charles play polo at a charity match in aid of the Police Convalescence and Rehabilitation Trust at the Guards Polo Club, Windsor Great Park on 14 June. The Queen (far left) had a smile for the Prince who was on the winning side. Meanwhile, Prince Henry (left above) and Prince William (left below) both enjoyed bowls of strawberries which they carried out of the tea tent. The following day, Monday the 15th, the annual Service of the Most Noble Order of the Garter was held at St George's Chapel, Windsor. The Order's procession from Windsor Castle to the Chapel draws the crowds each year. The Prince of Wales (right) is by tradition a Knight of the Garter and attended the Service with the Princess of Wales (below). This year the Queen invested the Duke of Kent and the Right Hon. Sir Leonard James Callaghan with the Insignia of Knights Companion of the Most Noble Order of the Garter. Traditionally the Garter is offered to former Prime Ministers on their retirement from politics but the only living Prime Minister in the Order in recent years has been Lord Wilson of Rievaulx until Sir James's historic honour.

On the morning of Saturday, 13 June, the Queen was present at The Queen's Birthday Parade on the Horse Guards Parade. (Left above) Queen Elizabeth, the Queen Mother, the Princess of Wales and Prince William drove to the Horse Guards Parade to see the ceremony. Afterwards the Queen (opposite below) drove back to Buckingham Palace at the head of the Queen's Guard. The Queen (right) with the Duke of Edinburgh and members of the Royal Family witnessed a fly-past by the Red Arrows, the Royal Air Force Aerobatic Team. (Below, left to right) The Duke and Duchess of York, the Princess of Wales and the Princess Royal (the title just bestowed on Princess Anne by the Queen) with (left to right) Zara Phillips, Prince Henry, Peter Phillips and Prince William on the balcony at Buckingham Palace.

Tuesday, 16 June saw the start of Ascot week and a royal fashion parade. For the first day (opposite above) the Princess of Wales wore a cream suit while the Duchess of York chose yellow. The second rainswept day (opposite below and this page) saw them, and the Princess Royal, in outfits of white, cream and navy blue.

Ladies' Day at Ascot is always a flamboyant occasion: the Queen Mother (left) as elegant as ever is loved by the crowds; Prince Charles (below) in the traditional royal procession at the start of each day's racing; and the royal ladies who chose the brightest and most fashionable colours for the day. The Princess of Wales (far right above and opposite below) wore a buttercup yellow suit splashed with a print of large flowers, by Bruce Oldfield, with a toning green hat by Philip Somerville. Princess Margaret (right) also chose yellow for her dress and jacket by Sarah Spencer. The Duchess of York (right and opposite below) wore emerald green with white spots – her dress of silk marocain was another Lindka Cierach creation (the designer of her wedding dress), and a hat by Graham Smith at Kangol completed the outfit. But for more serious racegoers perhaps the most interesting event of the week occurred the next day with Henry Cecil's success of seven winners during the 1987 Royal Ascot Races.

At 11 o'clock on 25 June, the Queen, accompanied by the Duke of Edinburgh, left Buckingham Palace escorted by a Sovereign's Escort of the Household Cavalry and travelled to the Palace of Westminster to open the new Session of Parliament. When the Queen arrived at the Houses of Parliament a 41-gun salute was fired by The King's Troop, Royal Horse Artillery, in Hyde Park, and at midday from the Tower of London by the Honourable Artillery Company. The Queen was received by the Lord Great Chamberlain (the Marquess of Cholmondeley) and the Earl Marshal (the Duke of Norfolk). Also present at the State Opening of Parliament were (far left above) the Duchess of Kent and (left above) Princess Margaret. (Far left below) The Imperial State Crown, together with the Cap of Maintenance and the Sword of State are carried into the Chamber for the State Opening. In the formal procession (this page) the Queen is followed by (left) the Countess of Cromer (Lady in Waiting), (centre) the Duchess of Grafton (Mistress of the Robes), and (right) Mrs John Dugdale (Lady in Waiting).

During the evening of 2 July (above left) the Duke and Duchess of York, Earl and Countess of Inverness, flew to Inverness in Scotland. They were received at Dalcross Airport by the Lord Lieutenant for Inverness. The Duchess then accompanied the Duke to Queen's Park where he opened the new spectator stand. The following day the royal couple visited Culloden Moor (above right), the scene of the battle of Culloden in 1746. The Earl and Countess of Inverness toured the Visitor Centre at Culloden where they enjoyed a display of audio-visual effects of the battle. They then walked to Old Leanach Farmhouse now restored as a battle museum. On 4 July (right) the Duke and Duchess of York travelled to York where they named a 125 train engine The Duke and Duchess of York, visited the Mansion House and the Enterprise Centre before receiving the Freedom of the City and then attended a service in York Minster. During the afternoon the royal couple toured the Castle Museum. It is the first time this century that a Duke and Duchess of York have visited the city officially.

Princess Margaret visited the London
Docklands Development Corporation at
12.45 p.m. on Wednesday, 8 July. The
Princess viewed the extensive works being
carried out by the Corporation in the
once redundant docklands and now the
scene of spectacular development. This
visit took place only three weeks before the
planned formal opening by the Queen of
the London Docklands Light Railway, the
£77-million construction which is 7½
miles long and the first phase of the new
railway.

THE DUKE AND DUCHESS OF YORK'S VISIT TO CANADA

15-26 July 1987

On the morning of Wednesday, 15 July, the Duke and Duchess of York left Heathrow Airport in an aircraft of the Canadian Armed Forces at the start of their visit to Canada. Their tour included Ontario, Manitoba, Alberta and the Northwest Territories. The couple were officially welcomed at Toronto's Queen's Park (above and top right) where vast crowds awaited them.

On 16 July the royal couple flew to
Thunder Bay and canoed up the river
(left) to the fur-trading post of Old Fort
William. Descendants of the fur folk
crowded the main square to welcome the
Duke and Duchess (left above). Later in
the day the couple attended a formal
dinner (above and above right) given by
the Canadian government at the Royal
York Hotel in Toronto. The next day the
Duke and Duchess (top right) visited the
Ontario Games for the Disabled where the
Duchess (top left) started a slalom heat.
That evening (right) the couple were taken
by police launch for a performance at the
concert hall of Ontario Place.

For thousands of years the Niagara River
has cut its way across the rock between
Lake Ontario and Lake Erie to form the
Niagara Falls – the spectacular Horseshoe
Falls and the American Falls. The Falls
have attracted many tightrope walkers
and stunt artists. Perhaps the highlight of
their Canadian Tour was the Duke and
Duchess of York's visit to Niagara Falls
(opposite page) during the afternoon of
18 July. The couple arrived by helicopter
to be welcomed by crowds of more than
100,000. They took photographs of the
Horseshoe Falls from Table Rock, perched
just above. After an official presentation
by the Mayor at the top of the 500-foot-
high Skylon Tower, overlooking the Falls,
the couple donned oilskins and boarded
Maid of the Mist III for a trip to within a
few hundred yards of the Falls. The
Duchess made straight for the bow to take
more photographs. On the return trip the
boat took the royal couple past the
American Falls. It was a memorable
afternoon. The following morning (this
page above) the Duke and Duchess flew
by helicopter to Coburg where they
attended Morning Service at the Church of
St Peter and a civic welcome which
included the dedication of the Duke of
York Square. That afternoon (right) was
spent at the Woodbine Racecourse in
Toronto where the 128th running of the
Queen's Plate took place. The Duchess
presented the porcelain cup to the winner
whose horse Market Control won the race
at 9-1 odds.

On Wednesday, 22 July, the Duke and Duchess of York flew to Winnipeg, capital of Manitoba, fourth city of the land and the ethnic centre of Canada (above left). They were officially welcomed at the Legislative Building and then attended a reception. Later in the day they flew 700 miles west to Edmonton in Alberta. The following morning the royal couple flew to Medicine Hat, a small town where they attended the official opening of the Medicine Hat Stampede (left). They rode into the stampede stand, saw wild horses in the corrals and watched some bronco-busting. Next on their busy itinerary was a trip to Fort Macleod and the opening of the Interpretive Centre at Head-Smashed-In Buffalo Jump Provincial Historic Site. With 5,000 years of history, pre-dating the pyramids, it is here that the plains meet the Rockies and Indians stampeded buffalo over the steep cliff. The couple were presented with a 60-lb stuffed bull's head (above right). The following afternoon (opposite) the Duke and Duchess toured Fort Edmonton, famous during the Gold Rush in the 1880s. The Duchess wore a cornflower blue dress of the period and the couple toured the streets in a wagon.

During the evening of Friday, 24 July, the Duke and Duchess of York (left) attended a dinner in Edmonton given by the Premier of Alberta. In the middle of his speech of thanks the Duke handed over the lectern to his wife, much to the delight of the audience. Two days later the couple visited Yellowknife, the capital of the North West Territories. The Duchess is seen here (above) arriving at the Giant Yellowknife Mine. There was a gold rush here in the 1930s but the boom did not last. Gold has been found once more and the mine employs 400 men. The Yellowknife miners presented the Duchess with a lump of ore as a wedding anniversary present.

On 27 July the Duke and Duchess (this page and overleaf) started a private holiday in the North West Territories – the land of the midnight sun where there is snow and twilight for eight months of the year. During the two-week canoe trip down the Thelon River the party slept rough under canvas and caught their own food.